NORTH CAROLINA
STATE BOARD OF EDUCATION
DE████████████████LEGES

P9-DFW-748

Bob Hope Master of Entertainment

Bob Hope Master of Entertainment

by Paula Taylor
illustrated by Harold Henriksen

Creative Education
Mankato, Minnesota 56001

Published by Creative Education, 123 South Broad Street,
P. O. Box 227, Mankato, Minnesota 56001
Distributed by Childrens Press. 1224 West Van Buren Street, Chicago, Illinois 60607
Library of Congress Numbers: 74-19116   ISBN: 0-87191-408-5
Library of Congress Cataloging in Publication Data
Taylor, Paula.   Bob Hope.
SUMMARY: A brief biography of the entertainer and comedian
emphasizing the events of his more than
forty-year career in show business.
1. Hope, Bob, 1903-   —Juvenile literature.
(1. Hope, Bob, 1903-   2. Humorists. 3. Entertainers)
I. Henriksen, Harold, illus. II. Title
PN2287.H63T3   790.2'092'4 (B) (92) 74-19116
ISBN 0-87191-408-5

INTRODUCTION

Among entertainers Bob Hope is unique. He has been a star in vaudeville, on Broadway, in films, on radio, and on television. No other comedian has mastered so many different mediums. For over 40 years his sharp wit has delighted small-town folks and New York sophisticates, GI's and generals, Presidents, and even a king. Through his 71 feature films, over 1,000 radio shows, and 300 television specials, Bob Hope has become an American institution.

Though he is now in his seventies, Bob Hope's popularity continues unmatched. At a Hollywood banquet in his honor, one speaker ended his tribute to Bob Hope with an old Irish saying, "May the Lord take a liking to you, but not too soon." Millions of his fans agree.

Bob**Hope**Master of
Entertainment

The contestants lined up. They wore oversized, battered shoes and derby hats and had penciled-in moustaches. One by one, they walked duck-legged onto the make-shift stage, rattan canes twirling in imitation of Charlie Chaplin.

When they'd finished their acts, the announcer held his hand over the head of each contestant in turn, cocking his head to judge the volume of applause. One small boy definitely was the audience's favorite. Bob Hope accepted the prize matter-of-factly. He wasn't surprised at winning — his brothers had rounded up the whole neighborhood gang to applaud for him.

To Bob, entering contests was just a way to earn money. He and his pal Whitey Jennings attended most of the employee picnics held during the summer by the large companies in Cleveland. Besides free food, there were always foot races for the children. Bob and Whitey entered all the races. The usually won first and second prizes. On a good Saturday, they sometimes pocketed as much as $25 each in prize money.

Most of the money Bob earned went into the family treasury. The Hopes were always short of funds. Over the years, Bob's father faced one business setback after another. In 1903 when Bob was born, William Henry Hope was a busy stone mason in Eltham, England. But building styles became simpler, and the ornate stone-cutting he specialized in went out of fashion. Mr. Hope's skill was less in demand. With time on his hands, he began stopping frequently at the local pubs. Soon he was spending more time at bars than on the job. He also began betting on the horses. Eventually, he lost everything.

In 1908, when Bob was 5, the family sailed to America to make a fresh start. They joined two of Mr. Hope's brothers in Cleveland. But things weren't much better there. Occasionally, Mr. Hope would be called to New York to put a stained glass window in a church, but jobs were few and far between.

To help make ends meet, Bob's mother began taking in roomers. The family moved several times into larger houses so that more roomers could be accommodated. All 7 boys helped out. At one point, Bob sold newspapers on one corner of a busy intersection. Three of his brothers had stands on the other 3 corners.

One of Bob's regular customers arrived every day in a chauffeur-driven limousine. This man never spoke. He counted his change very carefully and never tipped. Bob later found out that he was the millionaire, John D. Rockefeller, Sr.

Besides selling newspapers, Bob held a number of other jobs. At one time or another, he worked as a caddie, a shoe salesman, a soda jerk, a delivery boy, and a stock boy for an auto parts company. Sometimes he found a way to supplement his regular salary.

As a delivery boy for a bakery, he had to make the rounds of one of Cleveland's posh residential sections by streetcar. As he knocked on each door, he'd try to make himself look as pathetic as possible. He would tell the lady of the house, "Did I have a tough time finding this house!

I spent all my carfare looking for it." Feeling sorry for him, the soft-hearted housewife would give young Bob 15 cents carfare, which he promptly pocketed. His scheme worked fine, until one day he pulled the trick twice at the same house. The irate housewife reported him to the bakery, and Bob got fired.

Bob's antics must have caused his mother a lot of worry, but she never admitted it. Avis Townes Hope had great faith in all 7 of her sons. Each of them believed himself to be her favorite.

Having been a concert singer herself, his mother was sympathetic to Bob's theatrical ambitions. Once she took him to see Frank Fay, then one of vaudeville's top stars. A few moments into the performance, she turned to Bob and said loudly, "He's not half as good as you."

"Sh-h-h," Bob said, embarrassed. "Please, Ma."

But she insisted loudly, "I don't care — he can't sing or dance. You can."

By this time, people were staring at them, but Mrs. Hope stared back, defiantly.

Later, as a vaudeville star, Bob came back to Cleveland and played the same theatre. His mother sat in the front row, beaming. She wasn't surprised at his success — only that it took so long for everyone else to recognize his genius.

Although all the Hope boys sang, Bob's mother thought he had the best voice in the family. She gave him singing lessons at an early age. Before he sang on the stage, Bob

used to earn money singing on street corners, in front of
apartment buildings, and outside local bars and restaurants.
Later, he remarked that he wasn't quite sure whether the
people who threw coins at him appreciated his efforts or
were just bribing him to go away.

Bob much preferred singing to studying. He left high
school in his junior year to work at his brother Fred's meat
market. It wasn't that he was interested in the meat business.
(His brother once overheard him trying to sell a customer
a ham — while showing her a leg of lamb.) But he was
determined to go into show business and needed money
to do it.

With the money he earned at the meat market, Bob
took dancing lessons from a black entertainer named King

Rastus Brown. Then he started entering amateur contests. Except when his teacher was one of the contestants, he usually won the $10 first prize.

When he was 19, Bob and his girlfriend, Mildred Rosequist, worked up a dance act. They performed at several small theatres around Cleveland on Saturday nights. Encouraged by the success of their act, Bob decided to quit his job at the meat market and try his luck on the stage full-time. He planned to take Mildred with him, but her mother objected. She firmly believed that Bob would never amount to anything.

Bob heard that the manager of the Bandbox Theatre had engaged a high-priced star named Fatty Arbuckle. Several cheap acts were needed to round out the show. Hope and a friend, Lloyd Durbin, tried out for one of the spots. They got the booking. Besides several dance numbers, they sang "Sweet Georgia Brown" and did an Egyptian comedy routine in pantomime.

Their act was a success. Through Fatty Arbuckle, they were introduced to producer Fred Hurley, who found a spot for them in his touring show, the *Jolly Follies*. The company traveled south from Cleveland through several states, playing in small towns.

Working conditions on the small-town circuit were difficult. Hope's salary was only $40 a week. Bed was often a bus seat. At a performance, anything could happen — and often did. But it was on these small-town tours that Hope developed his unshakable poise in front of an audience.

After less than a year, the Hope-Durbin act ended in tragedy. After a show in Huntington, West Virginia, Lloyd stopped in at a local restaurant for a piece of coconut cream pie. Later he complained of stomach pains. He was rushed to the hospital, but it was too late. He died of food poisoning.

With a new partner, George Byrne, Bob went back on tour. The two began to experiment with comedy routines. In McKeesport, Pennsylvania, they tried one in blackface. The act went all right, but afterwards they found they had used the wrong kind of makeup. Instead of burnt cork, they'd put on black greasepaint. At 2:00 a.m. they were still trying to scrub the stuff off with very little success. They told the manager they thought they'd skip the blackface from now on — it cut down on their sleep. By the time they got to bed, it was time for the next show.

After 2 years on the small-town circuit, Hope and Byrne were still making only $50 a week. Then they were offered a booking in Pittsburgh at $300 a week. That engagement convinced them they had hit the big time at last. They decided to head for New York.

They polished up their act and invested in fancy costumes — top hats, canes, jackets with big white collars, high-waisted pants, and white spats. They even had their publicity pictures taken in the new outfits. But bookings in New York proved hard to get.

The two of them shared a tiny room in a sleazy hotel and existed largely on lemon pies sent by Bob's mother.

Finally, they got a part in a Broadway show, *The Sidewalks of New York*. The rest of the show got good reviews — but the Hope-Byrne act didn't. Their routine was cut. Bob and George found themselves back on the streets again.

In desperation, they worked up some new routines. When they finally got another booking, they invited a man from a talent agency to come and see their new act. He refused. He'd already heard about it. He advised them to head west and start over again. They took his advice and wired an agent in Cleveland who offered them a booking — but at the old salary of $50 a week. They accepted it gratefully.

Then Bob's luck changed. At the end of an evening performance in New Castle, Pennsylvania, he was asked to announce the next week's show: "Marshall Walker and His Big Time Review." Bob told the audience, "I know Marshall. He's a Scotsman. He got married in the backyard so the chickens could get the rice." That got a big laugh, so he told another joke — then another. Audience response was so good that the management made Bob's routine a regular feature of the show.

One of the orchestra members told Bob he ought to forget the double act with the dancing and become a master of ceremonies. Bob thought it over and decided to try working alone. He and George parted company.

After a few solo engagements in Cleveland, Hope felt confident enough to tackle Chicago. As in New York, he

had trouble getting bookings. Later, he quipped that during this period he was so unfamiliar with steak, he'd forgotten whether you ate it with a fork or drank it from a cup. He was so desperate, he even changed his name.

As a boy, he had suffered a lot of ribbing about his name — Leslie Townes Hope. "Les Hope" was quickly switched to "Hopeless" by mischievous schoolmates. In Chicago, he decided "Lester" sounded more masculine than "Leslie." Later, he changed "Lester" to "Bob," which he explained had more "Hi ya, fellas" in it.

But in Chicago, not even a new name helped the young comedian get bookings. Discouraged and $400 in debt, he was about to give up show business and go back home.

Then a friend got him a one-day job as master of ceremonies at a Chicago theatre. After the second of 3 shows that day, the manager of another theatre saw him and invited him to be emcee there.

At the Stratford, Hope was an instant hit. His engagement stretched from 2 weeks to 6 months. The salary of $300 a week solved his money problems. But success brought other worries. Many people in the audience came to the theatre twice a week. Jokes quickly became stale, forcing the aspiring comedian to tap every source of humor he could think of. He clipped jokes out of magazines. When new actors came in, he'd ask them if they had heard any good jokes.

During his run at the Stratford, Bob learned a lot about getting laughs. He'd lead off the act with a subtle joke and tell the audience, "Go ahead and figure it out." Then he'd stand there until they got it, even if the wait seemed endless. But he found audiences didn't like a comedian to be too smart. Sometimes he'd purposely tell a bad joke, make a wry face, and say, "I found that joke in my stocking. If it happens again, I'll change laundries."

After 6 months at the Stratford, the scramble for new material became too tiring. Bob teamed up with a Chicago girl named Louise Troxell and put together an act with the jokes he had accumulated. Bob and Louise went on tour on the Keith Western circuit, a notch below the big time.

But Bob wasn't satisfied. He still dreamed of success in New York. His goal was to play the top vaudeville house there — the Palace Theatre. He managed to get bookings at several other New York theatres. Then, at last, he was invited to play at the Palace in *The Antics of 1931*.

After opening night, the reviews were not very encouraging. One was openly hostile. It read: "If Bob Hope is the sensation of the Midwest, why doesn't he go back there?" Although disappointed by the reviews, Bob finished the engagement, which eventually led to an invitation to appear in a Broadway musical, *Ballyhoo of 1932*.

The night *Ballyhoo* opened, Hope's ability to ad-lib saved the show. The cast had trouble getting organized. The orchestra played the opening music twice. But still the curtain didn't go up. The audience was getting restless. Catcalls were heard. The producer was frantic.

Then Bob ran out on stage and started telling jokes. He looked up in the balcony and called, "Hello, Sam. That's one of our backers up there," he told the audience confidentially. "He says he's not nervous, but I notice he's buckled his safety belt."

There were a few snickers — then loud laughter. The crowd had been won over. Hope continued his rapid-fire quips for 5 more minutes. By that time, the actors were ready, and the show went on.

Bob Hope's impromptu routine was such a success that he was asked to open the show every night. But Broadway stardom didn't last long. *Ballyhoo* ran in New York for only about 4 months before it folded.

Two years later, Hope returned to Broadway in the Jerome Kern musical, *Roberta*. The story concerned a football star who owned a women's dress shop. Bob played the football player's pal, Huckleberry Haines. When the show opened, the producer decided it needed some extra comedy. Bob obliged with a number of gags which livened up the show and helped it enjoy a good run. He still regards *Roberta* fondly as his first success in show business outside vaudeville. He revived the show to open his 1958 television season.

After *Roberta*, Bob starred in the *Ziegfeld Follies of 1936* and several other Broadway productions, but more and more of his time was spent in Hollywood. His first movie was a short subject entitled, "Going Spanish." Hope wasn't happy with the picture. He said it was so bad that "when they catch John Dillinger, the current Public Enemy Number 1, they're going to make him sit through it twice." Unfortunately, his comment was quoted in a newspaper column, and the film's producer didn't think it was funny. That was Bob's last picture with that studio.

His first full-length movie, a musical revue called *The Big Broadcast of 1938*, was notable largely because of a number Bob sang called "Thanks for the Memory." The song got rave reviews and became Hope's trademark in later radio and television shows.

Of Bob Hope's 71 films, among the best are the *Road to Zanzibar* and the other *Road* pictures he made with Bing Crosby and Dorothy Lamour. The plots of all the *Road* movies were very much the same — Hope and Crosby escaping from zany predicaments while pursuing Lamour. But the story wasn't important. It was merely a backdrop for Hope's and Crosby's clowning.

While making the first *Road* picture, the pair did so much ad-libbing that the director was often sent flipping frantically through his script, searching for the lines they were saying. However, when he noticed the film crew doubled up with laughter at their antics, he decided not to hold them to the script. He told them he'd start the camera, and they could take it from there.

The director kept his word. Almost nothing was cut,

THE GHOST BREAKERS MOVIES

however bizarre. In the *Road to Morocco*, there was a scene where Bob had to walk up to a camel. As he did so, the camel spit in his eye. The scene was duly recorded and appeared in the finished film.

At the same time he was appearing on Broadway and making movies, Bob Hope was trying to break into radio, which was then a fairly new medium. He made brief appearances on a number of shows, but these weren't very successful. Bob found it difficult to tell his jokes into a microphone instead of playing to the audience.

Finally, in 1937, Hope signed a 26-week contract to appear on the Woodbury Soap Show. Just before the first broadcast, he discovered that no arrangements had been made for a studio audience. Frantically, he pleaded with the NBC program man to get him one. Talking into the microphone was bad enough. To have no audience reaction at all would be disastrous.

But Bob was told that it was too late to sell tickets and make other necessary arrangements. At the last minute, Hope found out the ventriloquist Edgar Bergen was broadcasting just before the Woodbury Show in an adjoining room. Bob persuaded an usher to rig the ropes so that Bergen's audience streamed out the exit directly into his studio. With his stolen audience, plus a few ushers and shoeshine boys he had bribed to show up, Hope got the laughs he needed. The premiere performance was a success.

A year later, Hope found a sponsor for a show of his own. The format of his show wasn't much different from many others of the day. In addition to Bob and his special guests, there was a band and a vocal group. There were also the "regulars," including a crazy professor, a female comic called Vera Vague, and Brenda and Cobina, who spoofed 2 currently-popular society beauties. But Hope's show was faster paced than any of its competitors. The comedian was once clocked at 7 jokes a minute.

Preparation for the show was grueling. Each of Hope's 12 writers had to prepare an entire script every week. The best jokes from each script were compiled for a 90-minute show which was played before a live audience and recorded. Hope would then select the best segments for the 30-minute radio show.

Bob's hard work paid off. In 1939 after *The Pepsodent Show* had been on the air one year, a poll showed that Bob Hope ranked fourth among radio's top comedians, behind Jack Benny, Fred Allen, and Edgar Bergen. The next year he ranked first.

Bob Hope's *Pepsodent Show* continued to get top ratings during the war years when it was broadcast with GI audiences from military bases around the country. But during the 50's, radio comedy audiences gradually diminished. More and more people were buying television sets. Hope's ratings fell. In 1953, his show was switched to a daytime slot, where it continued for 5 more years before going off the air. In all, Hope's radio shows lasted 20 years.

Having pioneered in radio comedy, Bob Hope was eager to try the new medium of television. In January, 1947, he appeared in the first commercial television broadcast in the western United States. Two years later, he made a surprise guest appearance on the Ed Sullivan Show.

Then, on Easter Sunday in 1950, he appeared in the first of his own shows, a musical comedy revue with a glittering cast of stars. The show was spectacular. So was the price. Hope was paid $40,000 for it — 4 times the amount ever paid to a single actor before. Bob played down his success. "I did my first television show a month ago," he told an audience, "and the next day 5 million television sets were sold. The people who couldn't sell theirs threw them away."

After almost 25 years, Bob Hope's TV specials continue to get top ratings. For them, he books top stars, not only in show business, but in other fields as well. In 1972, Olympic swimming star Mark Spitz and world chess champion Bobby Fisher were Hope guests. Bob feels the secret of his success is that he has avoided doing a weekly show. His television appearances have been limited to a maximum of 9 a season. As a result, he has outlasted all the other popular TV comedians who faded away after a few years, their humor dulled by the weekly grind.

Hope's TV appearances have not been limited to his own specials. In addition to many guest appearances, he has hosted a dramatic series, "Bob Hope Presents the Chrysler Theatre," and a variety of telethons, including one to aid victims of the Wilkes-Barre, Pennsylvania, flood in 1972. He also did a daily 5-minute radio and television commentary during the 1952 Republican and Democratic conventions. He has been master of ceremonies for the Academy Awards 14 times.

Bob Hope's Christmas Specials are among his most popular television shows. They regularly draw bigger TV audiences than any other specials on the air. The Christmas Specials are painstakingly compiled from thousands of feet of film, shot on Bob's annual holiday tours of American military bases overseas. His 1965 USO tour was a typical whirlwind affair. In 12 days, Hope traveled 23,000 miles, giving 24 shows at 18 different bases in Thailand and Vietnam.

Bob Hope has been dubbed "America's #1 Soldier in Greasepaint." In the 30 years he's been entertaining servicemen, he has traveled millions of miles, under conditions as hazardous as most GI's faced.

During World War II, when he was doing a USO show in Algiers, he was invited to meet General Eisenhower. As they chatted, Eisenhower remarked that Bob would be able to get a good rest that night. Algiers hadn't been bombed for over a month because the American artillery was so strong.

About 3:00 a.m., the air raid sirens sounded. Hope spent the rest of the night shivering in the hotel's wine cellar,

which had been converted to a makeshift air raid shelter. As the bombs exploded above him, he composed a wire to Ike, thanking him for the good night's rest. He added, "I'm glad I wasn't here on one of the nights when you had some action."

In Korea, Hope's USO troop once beat the Marines to the beach. When their plane landed at Wonsan Airport, they were surprised to find the place deserted. Finally, an admiral ran up, looking shocked at seeing them. He told them that when their plane landed, the airport had been surrounded by guerilla forces. The Marines were just then in the process of invading. When Hope did a show for the Marines who'd been in the invasion party, he told them, "It's wonderful seeing you. We'll invite you to all our landings."

During the Vietnam War, Hope was sometimes criticized for his support of American troops in a war many people felt the United States shouldn't be fighting. He responded by saying that, while he wasn't in favor of any war, he thought men in uniform deserved to be supported. His is a personal concern for the problems of ordinary soldiers. For them, he has done hundreds of radio shows without pay and visited thousands of sick and wounded men in hospitals.

More than any other entertainer, Hope has always been accepted as one of the troops. Soldiers double up with laughter at his digs at the top brass and the discomforts of military life. Bob easily adopts the mocking humor the soldiers prefer. He understands that even men facing death don't want sympathy. On entering a hospital ward filled with soldiers in traction, he is likely to quip, "Okay, fellas. Don't get up."

Occasionally, the GI's throw a dig right back at him. During World War II, he once came on stage wearing a dirty suit and a beat-up, dusty straw hat. He was limping and carrying a cane, having wrenched his knee jumping into a ditch during an air raid. The soldiers sized him up for a moment. Then someone yelled, "Hi ya, slacker!" Everyone, including Bob, cracked up.

Hope's ability to tailor his jokes to a particular audience and locale was particularly evident on his USO tours. At a base in Greenland, he told the GI's: "I'm very happy to be here at Thule. The temperature is 36 below. We don't know below what, the thermometer just went over the hill! ...We certainly got a wonderful reception when we landed. All those soldiers standing at attention! I understand they've been that way for 4 months!"

At a base on a lonely South Pacific island, he cracked: "Talk about remote . . . only the Navy knows whether these guys are stationed here or marooned!"

Bob's wife Dolores has long since resigned herself to his frequent absences from home, yet they have been happily married for 40 years. Being an avid golfer, Bob remarks that the length of their marriage is "four or five under par

for the Hollywood course." Bob gives Dolores the credit
for having maintained a normal family life for their 4 children, despite his hectic schedule and the glare of Hollywood
publicity.

Despite a personal fortune estimated at $500 million,
Bob Hope has never forgotten the lean years of his child-

hood. Now he is building a 2.5 million dollar mansion in Palm Springs. But for years, he opposed his wife's pleas for a home of their own. Eventually, he bought a modest, $30,000 home; and when the family outgrew it, he insisted on adding onto it, rather than buying a more expensive home.

Even today, a dinner break for Bob and his writers, who are among the highest-paid in the business, is likely to be a hamburger at a local drive-in. But in answer to those who would call him cheap, his friends are quick to point out his many benefit performances. Considering the $10,000 personal appearance fee he foregoes for each one, he sometimes gives away as much as $20,000 a week. At one point, he was doing so many benefits, one of his agents began calling him "Free Talent Hope."

One expense Hope doesn't skimp on is golf. He likes to be able to play a quick round of golf anywhere he goes. So he reportedly belongs to 15 or 20 different country clubs around the country, at a cost of $40,000 a year. He also has a private, one-hole golf course next to his house.

Hope shared his passion for golf with President Eisenhower and frequently played with him in Palm Springs. When Ike's health failed and he had to give up his favorite game, Bob cracked, "Of course, he paints a lot now instead of playing golf — it's fewer strokes."

Besides Eisenhower, Bob Hope has traded jests with England's King George VI and every United States President since Harry Truman. Although he often pokes fun at government officials, he is careful never to be cruel or too personal. Because of his tact, he has always been popular with the Presidents.

Most recently, he appeared at a banquet with former President Nixon. To the delight of news photographers, the two began comparing noses. (It's been rumored that Bob Hope's famous "ski snout" resulted from an accident, but Hope insists that's not true. He says it "came that way from the manufacturer.")

For his talent and contributions to various charitable and humanitarian causes, Bob Hope has received over 1,000 awards. Among them are the Medal of Freedom, the Congressional Gold Medal, the Purple Heart, and the Peabody award.

Now in his seventies, Bob Hope maintains a schedule that would tire most men half his age. Besides his TV shows, he does about 10 college shows a year and countless benefits. He pursues a whirlwind of activities, catching naps at odd moments on trains or planes or wherever he happens to be.

It's impossible to imagine Bob Hope retired, spending his days relaxing in an armchair in the sun. Maybe he never will. When questioned about retirement, Bob once replied that he'd still be getting laughs at his own funeral, "I've got a few jokes for the box. If they raise the lid, I'll say a few words."

Paula Taylor

Paula Taylor has only recently begun writing for young people. Having lived in 8 different cities, both in the U. S. and Europe, during the past 10 years, she has held a variety of jobs. She taught writing and literature to junior high school students in Wisconsin and California. In Iceland and the Netherlands, she taught adults basic English. In Athens, Georgia, she was a reader for the blind. A Phi Beta Kappa graduate of Carleton College, her interests range from horticulture to psychic phenomena. Presently, Ms. Taylor lives in Minneapolis, Minnesota with her husband and daughter.

Harold Henriksen

Harold was born in St. Paul, Minnesota and has lived there most of his life. He attended the School of the Associated Arts in St. Paul.

Even while serving in the Army, Harold continued to keep alive his desire to become an artist. In 1965 he was a winner in the All Army Art Contest.

After the Army, Harold returned to Minnesota where he worked for several art studios in the Minneapolis-St. Paul area. In 1967 he became an illustrator for one of the largest art studios in Minneapolis.

During 1971 Harold and his wife traveled to South America where he did on-the-spot drawings for a year. Harold, his wife and daughter Maria now live in Minneapolis where he works as a free lance illustrator.

Walt Disney

Bob Hope

Duke Ellington

Dwight Eisenhower

Coretta King

Pablo Picasso

Ralph Nader

Bill Cosby

Dag Hammarskjold

Sir Frederick Banting

Mark Twain

Beatrix Potter

close
ups